TABLE OF CONTENTS

Introduction

Reading books is an effective way to open our mind and learn new things. The second advantage of this activity is that it helps to improve writing and speaking skills. In addition, reading can also act as a method of stress relief. After a day up to your neck in work, it would be a good choice to enjoy a peaceful atmosphere by lying comfortably on the sofa and reading your favorite books. Sometimes, letting your mind free in the world of amazing stories is one of the best remedies for your day.

These brain teasers will challenge children and their parents to think and stretch their minds. There are have many benefits that they can get, such as:

Bonding – It is an excellent way for parents and their children to spend some quality time and create some fun and memorable memories.

Confidence Building – When parents give the riddles, it creates a safe environment for children to burst out answers even if they are incorrect. This helps the children to develop self-confidence in expressing themselves.

Improve Vocabulary – Riddles are usually written in advance words; therefore, children will need to understand these words before they can share the riddles.

Better reading comprehension – Many children can read at a young age but may not understand the context of the sentences.

Riddles can help develop children's interest to comprehend the context before they can share them with their friends.

Sense of humour – Funny, creative riddles can help children develop their sense of humour while getting their brains working.

QUIZ 1

1. My first home was a mine from where I was removed and stuck in the middle of hard wood. I can never escape and yet, you need me every day of your life. What am I?
2. My handbag is 35 cm in height and 40 cm in length. I have removed everything from it and it is now totally empty. I have coins measuring 2 cm in diameter. How many such coins can I put into my empty handbag?
3. To use me, you have to do this: Throw away the outside; cook the inside. Then eat the outside and throw away the inside.
4. You can never find these stones under the sea. What kind of stones am I talking about?
5. Which creature walks on 4 legs in the morning, 2 legs in the afternoon, and 3 legs at night?
6. This alphabet is the wettest of all. Which alphabet is it?
7. I belong to you and yet you never use me as often as other people use me. What am I?
8. I can be told, cracked, made, or played. What am I?
9. I have a thousand needles and yet I cannot sew or stitch.
10. What will happen when you remove the eye from the fish?

ANSWERS QUIZ 1

1. Pencil lead
2. Only one; because when you put in the first one, the handbag is no longer empty!
3. Corn
4. Dry stones
5. Man: crawls as a baby, walks on two when he is youthful, and uses a stick when he is old
6. C
7. Your name
8. A joke
9. Porcupine
10. It will become FSH

QUIZ 2

1. The yolk of an egg is white or the yolk of an egg are white?
2. Five men were on the road. Four were walking at the same speed and the fifth one was not. Yet, they all reached the destination at the same time. What is being described?
3. What has a bank but with no money? What has a bed with no mattress?
4. This boy had a wonderful red flashlight that burned quite bright. But one day, he buried it. Why did he do that?
5. It has four eyes that cannot see anything. And it flows beautifully murmuring often too.
6. I am my father's child and my mother's child. But I am no one' son.
7. There are nine dresses in the wardrobe and you take three to try on. How many do you have?
8. This alphabet is the longest of all. Which one?
9. I come once in a month, twice in a fortnight, but never in a hundred years. What am I?
10. I have a big family. My mother is the cloud. My father is the wind. My sons are the streams and rivers. My daughters are the seas and oceans. I finally rest on Earth. What am I?

ANSWERS QUIZ 2

1. Neither. Yolk is not white
2. Four pall-bearers carrying a coffin
3. A river
4. Because the batteries died
5. River
6. A daughter
7. 3(the rest are in the wardrobe)
8. Q (queue)
9. The letter 'T'
10. Rain

QUIZ 3

1. The name of this king begins and ends with five hundred. Five is right in the middle. First of all numbers and the first of all alphabets take up either place of the exact middle. Combine everything and you get a name that is the name of a great king. Name the king.

2. We are eight of us and we always move forward and never backward. We fight to keep our king safe from the attack of enemies. Who are we?

3. Two bodies on the floor are covered with broken glass and water. How did death occur?

4. This thing is rarely used in the day. It cries right through the night and sometimes dies by the time the morning comes. What is it?

5. A horse has a 25-foot chain around its neck. It wants to eat the hay that is 26 feet away. How will it be able to do it?

6. Steve loves to sleep like many of us. Yet, he manages to remain active and work well without sleeping for 9 days. How can this be?

7. This has a jacket but never wears trousers.

8. There is this amazing lady living in New Jersey who married four different men legally. Neither did she get a divorce nor an annulment. How did she manage it?

9. It has pointed fangs and pierces hard. It brings things together without losing a drop of blood.

10. This thing is great for serving but totally inedible.

ANSWERS QUIZ 3

1. DAVID
2. They simply throw one overboard making the boat one cigarette lighter
3. Bodies of two fish; the water and broken glass were from the aquarium that fell to the floor and broke
4. A candle
5. The horse is not chained to anything. It is free to walk wherever it wants
6. Steve sleeps only at night
7. Book
8. She was a minister
9. A stapler
10. Tennis ball

QUIZ 4

1. A squirrel, a bird, and a monkey are sitting on top of a coconut tree. A giraffe is standing close by too with its long neck ready to eat the banana. Which of the four will reach the banana first?
2. Sometimes doors are not doors. When?
3. I am a special kind of a coat that you can put on only when wet. Name me.
4. In the morning I lose my head but always get it back in the night. What am I?
5. Steve is in an open field with a ball in his hand. He throws the ball as hard as he can without bouncing it on any surface. After a few seconds, the ball comes right back to him. How is it possible?
6. This thing has a thumb and four fingers. But it is not made of flesh. What is it?
7. It has no voice and yet can cry. It has no wings and yet can flutter. It has no teeth and yet can bite. It has no mouth and yet can mutter. What is it?
8. I make things tight from one direction and make them loose from another direction. I turn and turn until the end is reached.
9. I have keys without locks. I have space without room. You can exit but never exit.
10. My name is Roger and I live on a beautiful farm with four other pups named Timothy, Tom, Tiger and Ranger. The farm is surrounded by green fields, beautiful tall mountains and a clear spring nearby. I love the farm I live on. What is the name of the fifth pup living on the farm?

ANSWERS QUIZ 4

1. Bananas don't come in coconut trees!
2. When doors are a jar!
3. A coat of paint
4. A pillow
5. He throws the ball in the upward direction
6. Fire
7. The wind
8. Screwdriver
9. Keyboard
10. Roger

QUIZ 5

1. Everything finishes with this. What is it?
2. This animal can jump higher than a castle. Which one?
3. Tom is a butcher who is 6ft 2in in height. He is slightly bulky in the middle. He wears leather boots right up to his knee. What does he weigh with his boots on?
4. I work at my best under pressure. The more pressure you put the better I become. In fact, without pressure, I am nothing. I am not easy to find. I am very hard too. What am I?
5. A microbe colony was founded by a single cell at around noon. This healthy microbe colony is lying in a petri dish. Every minute, each of the microbes is dividing into two. At exactly 12:33, the petri dish gets half full. At what time will the petri dish get completely full?
6. You need the following things to start a fire: petrol or kerosene or paper or candle and a matchbox along with a bit of cotton wool. What will you light first?
7. What goes up when it comes down and what comes down when it comes out?
8. Most people hate me but some people like me. I can change appearances and no matter how much you try to hide me, I will end up showing. I can never ever go down. What am I?
9. Dragons have to sleep all day. Why is that?
10. I reach for the skies and yet clutch the earth. I sometimes leave yet am around for a long time. Guess my name.

ANSWERS QUIZ 5

1. letter g
2. All animals can jump higher than a castle because a castle cannot jump
3. He is a butcher and so must be weighing meat
4. Diamond
5. The wise man simply told them to switch the camels.
6. Because the population of China is far greater than that of Japan
7. An umbrella (goes up with the rain comes down and goes down when the sun comes out)
8. Age
9. Because they fight (k)nights
10. A tree

QUIZ 6

1. There is a pond with a few lily plants. Each day, the lily pads become double in size. It takes 50 days for the pond to be half full. How will it take for the pond to be filled with lily?
2. I carry a lot of memories, but none of them are mine.
3. Two boys were born to the same mother at the same time, the same day, and the same year. Yet, these two boys were not twins. How is it possible?
4. With no arms, no feet, no wings, I still can climb towards the skies. What am I?
5. This letter is an important part of your head. Which alphabet is it?
6. This is a pair of words. One breaks but never falls and the other falls but never breaks.
7. This is round as a ring and flat as a leaf. It has two or four eyes but cannot see at all. What am I?
8. How many apples can grow on a tree?
9. April showers bring flowers. What do May flowers bring?
10. What falls down but is unbreakable?

ANSWERS QUIZ 6

1. 51; the next day, it will double again
2. A photo frame
3. They were two of triplets
4. Smoke
5. I (eye)
6. Day and night
7. Button
8. All apples grow on trees only
9. Pilgrims (the ship Mayflower)
10. Night (nightfall)

QUIZ 7

1. An eccentric king had a strange way of deciding the heir to his throne. He had two sons and only one could sit on it. He gave a camel to each of his sons and told them to ride out into the desert. The son whose camel comes second will be made the king. The sons are baffled and yet choose to ride the camels at extremely slow paces. After some hours of frustration, the two sons don't know what to do. They come across a wise man who gives them an idea and soon you could see them racing with each other towards the palace. What did the wise man say?

2. The height of Mount Everest was determined in 1856. Before that which was the tallest mountain in the world?

3. This question gets you different answers right through the day. Yet, all the answers are correct. What is the question?

4. Name any two keys that are good keys but cannot open any doors for you.

5. You and your sister leave from New York and Long Island respectively on two different buses on your way to your home in Connecticut. Your bus from New York travels at an average speed of 100 mph and that of your sister's travels at 120 mph. The buses meet at a point after a few hours of travel. Which of you is closer to your home?

6. It is round and short at the beginning and the end and high in the center.

7. What is the difference between a watchmaker and a jailer?

8. My belly is full. I am made of trees. With no feet but ready to roll, I love the water.

9. I am at the start of the end, I am in every second and every minute, and I am the end of life too.

10. Man and bottle have something in common. Can you guess what it is?

ANSWERS QUIZ 7

1. A pair of scissors
2. Survivors are not buried
3. What time is it?
4. Monkey and donkey
5. If the buses have met at the same point, both of you are at the same distance from home
6. Ohio
7. The watchmaker sells watches while the jailer watches his cells
8. A ship
9. The letter E
10. Neck

QUIZ 8

1. I am a parent but never nurse or birth. I am never still and yet never wander.
2. I have four fingers and a thumb just like you. And yet I am not alive. My partner is just like me; all fingers but no life. What am I?
3. I am filled with rivers, cities, towns, seas, oceans, mountains, and more. Yet, no one lives in these places. Who am I?
4. I put it up and it is bright. I put it down and it is dark.
5. Blue by day, black by night, I hold creatures in my site.
6. When you look at me, I show you.
7. I am light and float. More of me is hidden and only a bit of me can be seen.
8. The first letter is P and the last letter is E and it holds a lot of letters.
9. It has an eye that cannot see on one end and the other end is sharp
10. I am a letter of the alphabet that loves to ask for reasons. Which letter am I?

ANSWERS QUIZ 8

1. A tree
2. A glove (right and left gloves)
3. Map or atlas
4. Light switch
5. Seawater
6. Mirror
7. Iceberg
8. Post office
9. Needle
10. Y (why)

QUIZ 9

1. It can point in all directions but can never reach the destination on its own. What is it?

2. You are playing ping-pong with your friend and you are left with only one ping-pong ball. In some bizarre fashion, this ping-pong ball gets stuck inside a steel pipe that is embedded about 2 feet into a concrete floor. How can you remove the ping-pong without damaging it? You have the following tools at your disposal: your racket, your shoelaces, and a bottle of water.

3. Everyone loves to share this. But, once it is shared, it ceases to be what it is. What are we talking about?

4. Tim is alone in his house at night. The lights are off and it is so dark that nothing is visible. Yet, Tim is lying on the couch and reading a book. How is it possible?

5. These arrows from the heavens can never be counted and they do more good than bad for us. What are these arrows?

6. I am right at the end of a rainbow. What or who am I?

7. A window cleaner was working on the 45th floor of an apartment building cleaning windows there. He suddenly fell down but was unhurt. How?

8. What would you call a man who does not have all the fingers on one hand?

9. The power hat is given to me when the king is dead. The hat that is put on my head is very difficult to carry. Who am I?

10. Anybody can catch this. But no one can throw it. What is it?

ANSWERS QUIZ 9

1. Finger
2. He is a short man who cannot reach the 11th floor icon on the elevator. On the way down, he can easily reach the ground floor. When he has other people traveling with him, he can request the help of one of them to press the 11th floor. When he is carrying an umbrella, he can use it to reach the 11th floor button. At all other times, he can reach only the 7th floor button and get off and walk the balance number of floors.
3. A secret
4. Tim is blind and his book is written in 'Braille'
5. Rain
6. The letter 'w'
7. Because he was cleaning the windows from the inside of a home and he merely slipped on a drop of water and fell down on the floor. He got up and continued cleaning
8. Put on the first switch and keep it on for sometime. The bulb will become warm, right? Now, switch off this light and put on the second one. Now quickly go up the stairs. You can easily identify the bulb, which is connected to the second switch because it will be on right now. Now, touch the other two bulbs and see which is warm? That will be bulb of the first switch.
9. Prince
10. A cold

QUIZ 10

1. This comes in green too. But it is not a leaf. It copies others, but it is not a monkey. What is it?
2. The electric train is traveling in a southwesterly direction and a northeasterly wind is blowing in the area. Which direction is the smoke from the train traveling?
3. You can see through thick walls by having me by your side. What am I?
4. I may have a red hat and a stony heart. But I am still lovable.
5. When I'm still new and unused I am tall and as you keep using me, I become shorter and shorter. A mere breath is enough to kill me – Who am I?
6. This thing has no weight and if you were to put in an empty tin can, the can will become lighter than it was before. What are we talking about?
7. Although I have no life, I will always die.
8. I come where the rainbow ends and water begins.
9. I never ask questions and yet I am very often answered. What am I?
10. Steve is a huge football fan. He is so crazy about the game that he claims that he can tell the score even before the game starts. How is it possible?

ANSWERS QUIZ 10

1. A parrot
2. No smoke from an electric train
3. A window
4. Cherry
5. A Candle
6. The horizon
7. Batteries
8. The letter 'w'
9. The doorbell
10. You will light the match first

QUIZ 11

1. My second is formed by the first and my third is formed by the second and so forth. You can catch a thief with my help.
2. This group of three has one who sits and never gets up, the second who eats whatever you feed him, and the third who goes up never to return.
3. This is something that can be heard but can never be seen or caught.
4. There is a place where you are always silent. Which place?
5. What has plenty of teeth but never bothers to brush them?
6. It has a bark, but it cannot bite at all.
7. People need me most of the time to eat. However, they cannot eat me.
8. The one who makes me doesn't use me at the time he makes me. The one who pays the money to buy me does not need it for himself. The one who uses me doesn't even know he is using me.
9. I am found all over the world. I may be quite thin, but I am very important. You need me to learn. My parents are the forests. What am I?
10. Audrey's mother has 2 sons and 2 daughters. Her sons' names are John and Philip and one of her daughters is called Margaret. What is this lady's second daughter's name?

ANSWERS QUIZ 11

1. Footprints
2. Stove, fire, and smoke
3. Remark
4. A building ('u' is silent)
5. Piano
6. Tree
7. Plate
8. Coffin
9. Paper
10. Audrey

QUIZ 12

1. I am thin and beautiful. My roots are on top. I love the winters and hate the summers. A single ray of sunshine can kill me. What am I?
2. I run a lot and people hate it when I do. I stay in one place and yet my running annoys you.
3. This is a round box that has no key or lid. Yet, it holds a beautiful golden treasure inside it. What is it?
4. Without moving anywhere from a corner, this thing travels all over the round.
5. There is a man living in New York. Why can't he be buried in Chicago even if it is far away?
6. It remains only with me as long as I don't share it. Once I share it, it is not mine anymore. What is this?
7. This is yellow and looks like a half moon and has lots of seeds.
8. I am the most slippery nation in this entire world. Which country am I?
9. You are given two cups one with black tea and the other with black coffee. The liquids are equal in quantity. Now, you must take one tablespoon of black tea and pour it into the cup of black coffee. Mix well. Now, take one tablespoon of black coffee and pour it into the cup of black tea. Now, look carefully and tell which cup has more liquid.
10. Rolling cars, rising railroads, roaring lions! Can you spell that without any Rs?

ANSWERS QUIZ 12

1. An icicle
2. Running nose
3. An egg
4. Stamp
5. Because he is still living
6. A secret
7. Banana
8. Greece.
9. Both cups will have still have equal quantities of the liquid.
10. Yes, T-H-A-T. It has no Rs!

QUIZ 13

1. What comes between the earth and sun? Scientists are still struggling with this. Can you find it?
2. How will you read this out loud? I RIGHT I
3. A man lives on the 11th floor. He takes the elevator down every morning without fail. However, on his way back up, this is what happens: On rainy days or when he has other people traveling with him in the elevator, he goes up to the 11th floor. Otherwise, he goes up to the 7th floor and then walks up the balance 4 floors to reach his floor. Why does he do this?
4. A little girl and a doctor went to a rock-climbing camp. The girl was the doctor's child, but the doctor was not her father. What can the doctor be to the little girl?
5. I am the letter that can change your story into a building. Which letter am I?
6. You have two jugs of capacities 5 and 3 gallons each respectively. You have no other vessel or measuring device. How will you measure out 4 gallons from this setup?
7. This place has no east, west, or north and it is so cold that no man or beast can survive here. Which is this place?
8. One night, a king with his queen went to his place, which was completely empty. There was no one inside the palace or the courtyard or anywhere else. Yet, the next morning, three people came riding out of the palace. How?
9. Your school and your eyes have something in common. Can you guess what it is?
10. I always promise to come but never am today.

ANSWERS QUIZ 13

1. The word 'and'.
2. Right between the eyes
3. At 12.30
4. His mother
5. E (story becomes storey)
6. Fill the five-gallon vessel completely. Then, pour out two gallons from here into the 3-gallon vessel and then throw it out. After this, pour the leftover two gallons from the bigger vessel into the three-gallon vessel. Next, pour enough water into the big vessel so that it is completely full again. Now, you will have one gallon of space in the smaller vessel. Pour enough water from the big vessel to completely fill the small one. This will leave exactly four gallons in the big vessel.
7. Volume or temperature
8. Because the people who rode in were the (k)night, the king and his queen!
9. Pupils
10. Tomorrow

QUIZ 14

1. If you keep it, it will never break. But it is very difficult to keep it many times.
2. When you are looking for something, haven't you noticed that it is always in the last place that you look in? Why is that?
3. I am a six-letter word and if you took away one from me, I will become twelve. Which word am I?
4. Even the most intelligent people will overlook this thing. What?
5. A cowboy hangs up his hat and blindfolds himself. He then walks back 200 yards and aims for the aim and shoots right through it creating bullet holes. His blindfold is tamperproof ensuring he does see anything. How can he do it?
6. I am a word that looks the same if you see me upside down too.
7. A ladder is overhanging on the side of the ship. It has 20 rungs and the bottom-most one is just about touching the sea. There is a gap of 20 cm between every pair of rungs. Now, the tide rises at the rate 15 cm. When will the 6th rung (from the top) get fully submerged in water?
8. These arrows of God can never be counted
9. I live in a beautiful yellow single storied home with yellow walls, yellow floors, yellow cupboards, yellow carpets, yellow cushions, yellow curtains and everything else in yellow. What color are the stairs in my home?
10. I start quite ugly. But soon, I emerge beautiful and colorful and flutter away to the onlooker's delight.

ANSWERS QUIZ 14

1. A promise
2. Because when you find what you are looking for, you will stop looking
3. Charcoal
4. Their nose
5. He hangs his hat on his gun
6. SWIMS
7. Never, if the rising tide is lifting the ladder, it is also lifting the ship at the same rate.
8. Sun's rays
9. It is a single story home with no stairs
10. Butterfly

QUIZ 15

1. Is there a law against a man to marry his widow's sister?
2. Made of bone or metal and full of teeth, the ladies of the world love me.
3. It is something I have if I don't share it and don't have when I share it.
4. This is quite easy to get into for most of us. But we struggle to get out of it.
5. This brave goose fights with snakes. Which one?
6. This thing stays in its own place even when it goes off. What is it?
7. Who uses cowhides the most?
8. One night, a butcher, a baker, and a tradesman go to the hotel for dinner. When the bill comes, it is for four people. How is it possible?
9. When you buy me, I am black. When you use me, I turn gray. When you throw me, I am gray. What am I?
10. Name this thing: it has 'kst' in the center, in (at the start) and (at the very end)

ANSWERS QUIZ 15

1. Only half the way; because when he is on the other half of the field, he is running out of the field
2. A comb
3. Secret
4. Trouble
5. A mongoose
6. Gun
7. The cows themselves
8. Because there were four people including the (k)night
9. An echo
10. Inkstand (kst in the middle, in (at the beginning), and (at the end)

QUIZ 16

1. Three men were rowing a boat. They had four cigarettes among them. But, they had no match. How did they manage to smoke?
2. There is one letter in this sentence that is misspelled. Which is that word?
3. I cover your body, but I am not your clothes. The more you use me the thinner I get and the cleaner you get. What am I?
4. Everyone and everything has this and this thing can never be lost. What is it?
5. We are family of 12. I come second and yet I am the smallest. How is it possible?
6. You have to add 20 to the number 100. How many times can you do it?
7. This alphabet is always buzzing around. Which alphabet is it?
8. This thing has many eyes and yet it cannot see. What is it?
9. I bring about darkness even I force open an opening. The hyena, hippo and the horse know me, but spiders and snails don't know me. What am I?
10. This is what you can keep only if you give it away.

ANSWERS QUIZ 16

1. Mushroom
2. The word 'misspelled'
3. Bar of soap
4. Shadow
5. The family is the 12 months of the year. February has the least number of days and therefore the smallest.
6. Only once; because after that 100 will become 120
7. B
8. A hole
9. A yawn
10. Your word.

QUIZ 17

1. Give me the names of three consecutive days but without using Tuesday. Thursday or Saturday

2. When I am young, I'm sweet. In my middle age, I am better. But when I am old, I'm the best.

3. You can actually put something into a wooden box and still make it lighter than before. What can you put?

4. There was this beautiful sunny day when Tom was looking out into the harbor and saw a ship that was sinking. There was no storm or rain and yet Tom saw that the ship was sinking and went straight down. What was happening?

5. There are four horses, six dogs, and you in a barn. How many pairs of feet are there in the barn?

6. Made of carbon and water, I fizzle and sizzle. Kids love me.

7. I come from an egg. I have powerful muscles but no legs. I have a backbone too. I am quite long. And yet I can fit into a hole. Most importantly, I sizzle like bacon.

8. I am black seeds on white land. I see things.

9. A farmer had some peas and some potatoes to take to the market to sell. But, since he had only one bag and he didn't want to mix the peas and the potatoes, he first put the peas into the bag and tied it at the center. On the top portion, he put in the potatoes. Now, at the market, a man comes to him and says, "I only want the peas and not the potatoes." This man is carrying his own bag. Nothing can be dropped on the floor as the vegetables can get soiled. Trading bags or making holes is not allowed. How will the farmer transfer the peas from his sack to that of the buyer's sack?

10. I am a four-legged creature with no tail. I can be heard only at night. I love to jump.

ANSWERS QUIZ 17

1. Yesterday, today, and tomorrow
2. Wine
3. You can put holes
4. The submarine captain was ordering his crew to lower the vessel into the sea
5. Only your pair of feet because horses have hooves and dogs have paws
6. Soda pop
7. A snake
8. An eye
9. First, the farmer puts the potatoes into the buyer's sack and binds it tightly. Then he turns the buyer's sack inside out and fills it with the peas. He then unbinds the buyer's sack and transfers the potatoes back into his bag.
10. Frog

QUIZ 18

1. It has a neck that is used to name a traffic block. But on the neck, there rests no head.
2. You have 20 apples and 13 girls to distribute equally among. How will you do it in such a way that no girl gets more or less? The apples are equally distributed.
3. You can always count on these while doing math puzzles. What are they?
4. This thing is some distance away. It is possible to see it and move towards it. Yet, the distance will always remain. What is it?
5. Whether you use me to buy something or deliver me somewhere or smell me, I sound the same. What am I?
6. Five men were walking towards the church when it started raining heavily. Four of the five men ran for cover and yet got wet. The fifth man remained dry despite being in the rain. How is this possible?
7. With me, you can see through things very easily.
8. Imagine this: you are filling the bathtub in a completely locked airtight bathroom with absolutely no doors or windows. The bathtub tap suddenly breaks and the tub is overflowing filling up the floor and slowly the entire bathroom. You will soon drown. What will you do?
9. This is a fairly big tree, but you can easily carry it in your hand. What is this tree?
10. This thing is most often full the entire day and empty always at night. What is it?

ANSWERS QUIZ 18

1. Bottle
2. Simple; make apple juice and divide the juice equally among the 13 girls
3. Mount Everest only! Just because humans took time to read its height, doesn't mean it was not always so tall!
4. A glove
5. Cent, sent, and scent
6. The four men were pallbearers and the fifth man was the dead body in the coffin they were carrying
7. X-rays
8. I will stop imagining
9. A palm
10. Your shoes

QUIZ 19

1. I point in the correct direction and if you don't follow me, you can get punished. I have two words. (Clue: you find me on the roads)
2. I am used for drinking coffee. I am also a stop and can make others stop.
3. The ages of a father and his son total to 66. The numbers representing the ages of the father and son are reversed. What are their ages? (Clue: There are more than one answer to this riddle)
4. A farmer sent his son to the cattle market with $100 and told him to buy exactly 100 animals. There were goats, chickens, and rabbits for sale. A goat cost $10. A chicken cost $0.50. A rabbit cost $5. The farmer's son had to buy at least one of each animal. How does he do it?
5. A lady has six brothers and each of them has a sister. How many children does the lady have?
6. I come in a wide range of colors and you will see me almost everywhere. Look up and I'm sure you can see me. (Clue: I need to be wet to be put on)
7. You take this away from there and it comes here. What is it you take away?
8. This is a room that no one can enter and there is always no room here. What kind of room can this be?
9. The Wilson family were very wealthy and lived in a huge, beautifully done up, circular home. Mr. Wilson was a stickler for cleanliness. He woke up one morning and found a stain of jam on the table. He spoke to everyone. I was playing basketball – said little Wilson. I was sewing in my room – said Mrs. Wilson I was dusting the corners the house – said the maid. Who was lying?
10. What are the two things that can see what the other sees but cannot see each other at all?

ANSWERS QUIZ 19

1. No Way sign
2. Brake/break
3. Any of the following three will be taken as the right answer: 60+6, 51+15, 42+24
4. He buys one goat at $10. He buys nine rabbits for $45. He buys 90 chickens for $45. He spent $100 ($10+$45+$45) and gets 100 (1 goat + 9 rabbits + 90 chickens) animals.
5. Seven
6. Paint
7. The letter 'T'
8. This is not a legal question. If his wife is a widow, isn't he dead and if he is dead, where is the question of marriage
9. The maid. There are no corners in a circular home
10. Dozens

QUIZ 20

1. Four children, a dog, and the mother of the four children were walking holding a small little umbrella. Yet, none of them got wet. How?
2. With beautiful white fleece, I follow Mary everywhere she goes. I can be eaten too
3. They love the night and come out without even an invitation. They are not so fond of the day and disappear without telling us. What are they?
4. This thing is black or sometimes white too. This thing takes you where you need to reach someday but never brings you back. What is it?
5. Joel's mum has four ids. Their names are April, May, June, and

   ____

6. In the forward direction, I am very heavy. But, in the reverse direction, I am not. What am I?
7. The more you have of me, the more difficult it is for you to see. What am I?
8. Complete the sequence: MTWT…
9. I am loaded with keys of varying sizes and shapes and yet none of them can be used to open a single door. What am I?
10. We put this on the table and cut it many times. Yet, it cannot be eaten. What is it?

ANSWERS QUIZ 20

1. Because it was not raining
2. A lamb
3. Stars
4. A hearse
5. Joel
6. Ton (reverse is 'not')
7. Darkness
8. FSS; first letters of the days of the week starting from Monday
9. A piano
10. A pack of cards

QUIZ 21

1. Dog catchers get paid by the ___________
2. This kind of ship needs two mates but has no captain. What kind of ships are we talking about?
3. It is yours, but you hardly use it.
4. Anyone can hold this thing without the need for hands. Yet, no one can do it for long. What is it?
5. A man was carrying wood on this head, which was neither straight nor crooked. What kind of wood was it?
6. Just one word fits perfectly into each sentence. Which one? It is bigger and better than God. It is worse than demons. It is available in plenty to the poor people. The one who consumes it will certainly die
7. This happens to everyone at the same speed. What?
8. Your uncle's sister is not your aunt. So, what is she to you?
9. I am fine and powerful. I can build castles. I can bring down mountains. I can blind people and yet help a few people to see.
10. I am hairy and scary. I stand in the middle of nowhere. Scaring away others is my job.

ANSWERS QUIZ 21

1. Pound
2. Relationships
3. Your name
4. A potato
5. Sawdust
6. It is 'nothing'
7. Growing older
8. Your mother
9. Sand
10. Scarecrow

QUIZ 22

1. Is an old five-dollar note more than valuable than a new one?
2. It is usually a big green house that covers a white house. Inside the white house, there is a red house that is filled with black babies. What is it?
3. I have legs, a strong back and two good arms as well. Yet, I don't walk nor move around. What am I?
4. Unlike a knife that gets blunter with more use, I get sharper with more use. What am I?
5. This turns all things around and does it without moving. What is it?
6. Take away the head, it goes higher. Put the head, it goes lower.
7. This has a horn but cannot honk. What is it?
8. If a plane crashed at the border between Mexico and the US, where would the survivors be buried?
9. Why do Japanese men and women eat more rice than Chinese men and women?
10. I am a small house full of meat. I have no door or window for you to get in. You will have to break my walls down for that.

ANSWERS QUIZ 22

1. Of course, $5 is always worthier than $1 (new one)
2. A watermelon
3. An armchair
4. Your brain
5. Counterfeit money
6. Pillow
7. A rhino
8. He is still living
9. The man is normal. It wouldn't be nice to have all ten fingers on one hand, would it?
10. A nut

QUIZ 23

1. You are sitting on the bridge watching a boat filled with people coming towards the shore. As it comes slowly, you realize that there is not one single person on the boat. How is it possible?
2. Even though I have innumerable legs, I cannot stand straight. I have to only lean. You make me dirty so you can feel squeaky clean. What am I?
3. What has two head, six legs, two hands, and four ears? Remember it walks only on four legs.
4. There are four masters in this collection. One is a master of gems. The second is the master of hearts. The third is a master of big sticks and the fourth is a master of shovels. Who are the four?
5. Always full when you see her and yet nothing comes out of her, she is white, round, and beautiful.
6. I am a 6-letter word and I am secure and strong. Take away the head and I become an eating or meeting place. Take away the head again and I am ready's partner. Put both my heads back and I become an animal shelter.
7. This thing binds two people and yet touches one only.
8. You have this thing inside you that can be broken without anyone touching it.
9. This comes once every minute, two times a moment, and but once even once in a thousand years. What is this?
10. I have feet but no legs to speak of. Who or what am I?

ANSWERS QUIZ 23

1. All the people on the boat are married men and women.
2. A broom
3. A rider on horse
4. The kings in a deck of cards
5. Full moon
6. Stable
7. A wedding ring
8. Your heart
9. The letter 'm'
10. A snail

QUIZ 24

1. We are brothers who make something whole and yet we never meet. Who are we?
2. I live in every nook and corner of your body and I am also used unfailingly in any market. I am the same and yet different. What are my two versions?
3. We have our own two legs but nothing else. We are not made of flesh. We come in different colors and shapes.
4. This question can never get a response of yes.
5. Using only 8's, how can you get 1000 as the total? You can only add. You cannot subtract or multiply or divide.
6. I am a 5-letter word and I am very strong. Take away two letters and I become single. What word am I?
7. Here is the sequence of events: The rooster first laid 12 eggs, which the farmer took away. Then it laid another 7 eggs, which again the farmer took away. Finally, it laid 3 eggs. How many eggs did the farmer get?
8. Friday, Peter and Tom went for lunch and when the bill came, neither Peter nor Tom paid. Who paid?
9. I am all around the wood but not a bit of me is inside. What am I?
10. She had just learned to drive. She went down on a one-way street and was seen by the cop and yet he did not penalize her. How?

ANSWERS QUIZ 24

1. Day and night
2. Cell and Sell
3. Pants
4. Are you sleeping?
5. $888+88+8+8+8 = 1000$
6. Stone
7. Roosters don't lay eggs!
8. The third friend, Friday
9. Bark of a tree
10. Because the new driver was walking down the one-way street

QUIZ 25

1. This thing is so delicate that simply naming it can break it. What are we talking about?
2. I am a natural pathway that is located between high natural masses and if you remove one letter from me, you have an artificial pathway between manmade masses. What am I?
3. I can run down a slope easily. However, I cannot walk. What or who am I?
4. You can whip and beat this thing until it becomes hard. Yet it will not shed a single tear.
5. What can go up or down without moving an inch?
6. If you keep me warm and cozy, even without bones and legs, I will one day walk away from you.
7. Where do people chirp?
8. Poor people have me. Rich people don't have me. You will die if you eat me.
9. Numbers 88, 69 and 11 have something in common. Can you see it?
10. This animal loves doors.

ANSWERS QUIZ 25

1. Silence
2. Valley
3. Water
4. Cream
5. A mirror
6. Egg
7. On Twitter
8. Nothing
9. All three of them look the same upside down as well
10. Doormouse

QUIZ 26

1. When you break me, there is no noise.
2. Round and small, I am served at a table by two or four. I am hit back and forth and you will love me.
3. A little boy was climbing down a 25-foot ladder and suddenly he fell down. But the boy was not hurt. How is it possible?
4. I am everything to one person and nothing to another person.
5. I look and act like a cat. But I am not a cat. What am I?
6. I usually last for a few hours. When thin, I am very fast and when fat, I am a bit slow. A breath of air is my foe.
7. Which alphabet is not me?
8. Everyone has this dress. But no one can wear it.
9. I am lighter than a feather and yet the strongest man in this world cannot hold me for more than a minute or two. What am I?
10. I am full of puzzles. Some people have managed to solve some of my puzzles and yet there are millions more left to the solved. I am both adored and feared.

ANSWERS QUIZ 26

1. Promise
2. Ping pong ball
3. He was on the last step when he fell down
4. Mind
5. Kitten
6. A candle
7. U
8. Address
9. Breath
10. Math

QUIZ 27

1. The more it dries, the more it gets wet. What is it?
2. I am as light as a feather. I am, in fact, lighter than air. Yet, the strongest man in this world cannot lift me. Who am I?
3. Although water is life on this earth, that is the one thing that will kill me almost immediately.
4. Two ladies were standing facing opposite directions. One was facing east and the other was facing west. Yet, they were able to see each other. How is it possible
5. My face is full of numbers and yet you will not find thirteen. What am I?
6. This thing stalks you by day and leaves you alone at night.
7. There is one way a leopard can change its spots. How?
8. This only goes up and never comes down; no matter what.
9. Which insect is the best at gaming?
10. Although I don't have ears, eyes, tongue, or nose, I can hear, see, taste, and smell everything? Who is this all-in-one?

ANSWERS QUIZ 27

1. A towel
2. A bubble
3. Fire
4. They were holding mirrors
5. A clock
6. Your shadow
7. By moving from spot to spot
8. Your age
9. A cricket
10. Your brain

QUIZ 28

1. The answer to this question may be yes, but it actually means no. What is the question?
2. Name two perennial veggies that can grow for several years after you have planted them once unlike other veggies, which have to be replanted every year.
3. Hank was an old and tired man who rode into the village on Friday. He was so tired that he booked himself into an inn and rested for three days. He again left on Friday. How?
4. A man and his son were involved in an accident and were taken to two different hospitals. The son's doctor looked at him and said, "I cannot operate on this boy because he is my son." How is this possible?
5. This has no middle, no end, no beginning. And it's simply delicious too.
6. You will find me in villages, town, cities, and in all places outside but never inside. What am I?
7. There are 12 people running a race and you have just managed to overtake the boy who was running in the 4th position. What is your position now?
8. This runs around the house and also around a field. But, it remains stationary. What is it?
9. How many different kinds of species of animals and birds and plants did Moses take on his beautiful Ark?
10. I can appear from here to there and disappear from there to here.

ANSWERS QUIZ 28

1. Do you mind?
2. Rhubarb and asparagus
3. Friday was the name of Hank's donkey
4. Because the doctor was the mother of the boy
5. Doughnut
6. Streets
7. Fourth
8. A fence
9. None. It was not Moses' Ark. It was Noah's.
10. The letter T

QUIZ 29

1. A farmer has 30 sheep, 10 cows, and 15 pigs. If you call the cows as pigs, how many pigs will he have?
2. Even the dictionary spells this word incorrectly. Which word?
3. There is water running down a hill. When will it stop?
4. If you happen to know me, then I feel like nothing. But if you don't know me, I can be puzzling.
5. I am always in the arriving mode but never actually come.
6. I am weak and strong too. I have little powers and yet I am powerful.
7. I adore you and even though I show you my tongue, I am never ever rude to you.
8. Imagine you are in a dark and dingy room and suddenly you hear eerie noises. You also red eyes and teeth like that of the vampire you read in the story yesterday. The door is locked from outside. There are no other doors or windows. How will you get out?
9. You have drawn a line on a paper. Your friend comes and does something to make this line bigger. However, she does not touch or make changes to your line in any way. How did she do it?
10. This is a vehicle that has wheels and flies too. But it is not an aircraft. What vehicle is it?

ANSWERS QUIZ 29

1. 15 pigs only, you can call it by any name but it will remain a cow
2. The word 'incorrectly'
3. When the water reaches the bottom
4. A riddle or puzzle
5. Tomorrow
6. Emotions
7. A dog
8. Just stop imagining
9. She drew a line that is shorter than your line next to it.
10. A garbage truck

QUIZ 30

1. This alphabet can be very, very hot. Which one?
2. Which moves faster: heat or cold?
3. Black when clean; white when dirty; what is it?
4. You can drop me from the tallest building in the world and yet I will not die. But, put me in water and I am gone. What am I?
5. I run all around the meadow but am very still too.
6. How many oranges and apples can you put into an empty bag?
7. Who is the most silent Member of Parliament?
8. There is only one anagram of trinket. Can you find it?
9. A pregnant mother already has 6 children whose names are Doreen, Regina, Melanie, Fabby, Sonny and Larry. Use logic and tell me what will she name her seventh child: Archie, Benny, Tinny or Rosy?
10. This thing is not alive, has no lungs, and yet needs air for survival. What is it?

ANSWERS QUIZ 30

1. T (tea)
2. Heat; because everyone can catch a cold
3. Blackboard
4. Paper
5. Fence
6. Only one; because after the first one is put, the bag is not empty any more
7. The letter 'I' because it is not pronounced in 'parliament'
8. Knitter
9. Tinny; look at the names of her first 6 six children. They all start with do, re, me, fa, so, and la. So the last one will last with ti
10. Your fingers

QUIZ 31

1. I am filled with T. I start with T. I end with T and I am full of T. What am I?
2. I live in the center. Even I am broken, I can continue to work. If you want me to love you, you simply need to touch me. Yet, I am the most powerful thing in you.
3. What is common between dogs and trees? One makes a noise about it and the other gathers its strength from it.
4. I add four to nine and I get the answer as one. How is it possible?
5. A man drives his car all the way to the bank and shouts out loud, 'I am bankrupt.' Why does he do it?
6. I am a word that has to be pronounced wrong.
7. What has a tail, six legs, four eyes, and two heads?
8. You will always find me meandering outside whether rain or shine. I never once step inside any house.
9. I am a very lonely word and I am 5 letters long. You take away one letter and I am still lonely and if you take away another letter, I am still solitary. What word am I?
10. I have three full feet and yet I cannot walk or run or play. What am I?

ANSWERS QUIZ 31

1. A teapot
2. Your heart
3. The bark
4. I add four hours to 9 o'clock and the answer is one o'clock
5. Because he is playing the game, Monopoly
6. The word 'wrong'
7. A man riding a horse
8. Street
9. Alone
10. A yardstick

QUIZ 32

1. A crook brought me a coin, which had an embossing on it saying it was made in 200 B.C. I knew immediately this was a fake. How did I know?
2. This thing has plenty of teeth but cannot eat at all. What is it?
3. This thing has two brothers living together. If one is lost, then the other is useless. What is it?
4. I can run along merrily. But I don't know how to walk. I murmur many a time, but I don't know how to talk. I have a bed, but I do not sleep on it. What am I?
5. I am a tool that is more powerful than a sword or gun. Yet, I come very cheaply and you can buy men in a store.
6. You also have them and use them to wring with woe, hoe a row, and slay a foe.
7. When you take my skin off of my body, I never cry. But you will cry a lot. What am I?
8. This room has no doors and windows. What room is it?
9. Which part of London can you find in France?
10. I have four legs and a flat face. People use me always yet I never tire. I am always ready for work whenever you are. I usually have another 4-legged partner

ANSWERS QUIZ 32

1. The concept of B.C, (Before Christ) came into being only after Christ was born. How did the people know about B.C. during that time?
2. A comb
3. Breath
4. A river
5. Pen
6. Hands
7. An onion
8. A mushroom
9. The letter N
10. Desk

QUIZ 33

1. This fellow is my best friend because he is always there to take care of my mistakes. Who is he?
2. There are three bulbs in the upstairs room and their corresponding switches are on the ground floor. Now, you need to identify which switch is for which bulb. The restriction is you can climb up the stairs only once to check. However, you can put on or off a switch any number of times and for any duration of time. How will you identify which switch is connected to which bulb?
3. Everyone loves to give this away. Many people need it too. However, rarely do people use it themselves. What is it?
4. I am a word that means hardly there. If you take away my head, I become a great-smelling herb used in cooking.
5. I am this juicy fruit that can be red, green, or yellow
6. You already know that one is company and two is a crowd. Then, what are four and five?
7. These have a bottom right on top of them. What are they?
8. The only veggie that is not frozen or canned and is always sold fresh
9. Where do fishes keep their cash or money?
10. I can be seen in water. But I never get wet.

ANSWERS QUIZ 33

1. An eraser
2. All the other tools are red herrings. Simply pour water into the pipe until the ball floats up to the top.
3. Advice
4. Sparsely (parsley)
5. Apple
6. 9 (4+5)
7. Your legs
8. Lettuce
9. In the bank of the river
10. Your reflection

QUIZ 34

1. With lots of eyes and round or oval-shaped, I am loved by nearly everyone in this world. You can boil me or cut me into pieces and fry me and I turn out yummy.
2. This musical instrument is something you can only hear but never touch or see. Which is it?
3. You should throw me down if you want to use me and take me in when you don't want to use me.
4. What compels you to answer but never questions?
5. I am liquid and yet can make beautiful things. You push me too far and I will leave behind a big scar.
6. How will you share 5 apples that are in a basket among five girls with one apple still in the basket?
7. This has roots that no one can or has seen. It is taller than trees. It keeps on moving upwards and yet it does not grow. What is it?
8. This is the name of an insect. The first part of this insect is another insect. What are the two insects being spoken of?
9. Steve puts his hand into his pocket. It has nothing and is totally empty. Yet, Steve finds something. What does he find in his empty pocket?
10. I am an odd number. But, if you took away two letters from me, I become even. What number am I?

ANSWERS QUIZ 34

1. Potatoes
2. Your voice
3. Anchor
4. The telephone
5. Glass
6. Give one apple each to four girls and the apple that is left to the fifth girl along with the basket
7. A mountain
8. Beetle
9. A hole
10. 11 (take away e and l and you are left with even)

QUIZ 35

1. You plunge a knife into my heart and twist and turn and I open my heart to you.
2. It is as round as a ring and so deep that even all the horses of the king cannot pull it up. However, it has something sweet at the bottom that you can pull up. What is it?
3. I am a vehicle and whether you spell me forwards or backward, I remain the same. What am I?
4. I am a little seed in a green jacket. Stupid people are called by my name. Eat me raw and you will get a stomach ache.
5. This vegetable is very bad for ships. Which one?
6. Whoever makes these things does not tell, those who don't know these things will take it, and those who know about these things will not touch it with a barge pole. What are we talking about?
7. I have no siblings and yet, this man's father is my father's son. Who are we talking about?
8. This thing flies all around and all day but still never leaves its place. (Clue: People sometimes sing a special song as it flies around)
9. Everyone in the world including highly learned scholars pronounce me wrong. Who am I?
10. With a sunny and yellow disposition, I have a black eye in the middle. I am attached strongly down and yet follow my king as he moves around. What am I?

ANSWERS QUIZ 35

1. Lock
2. A well of water
3. RACECAR
4. Peas (pea-brained)
5. A leek (leak)
6. Your eyes
7. The man himself
8. Flag
9. The word 'wrong'
10. A sunflower

QUIZ 36

1. This thing is as big (and sometimes, bigger) as an elephant. But it has no weight.
2. Without speaking or listening, I always say the truth. Who am I?
3. This thing claps so loudly that many, many people can hear it. But it has no hands.
4. A dog runs into a field at great speed. How far can he run into the field?
5. I am a word of three letters that means a little. You add two letters and I become even littler. What word am I?
6. There are 29 apples in a bowl on the dining table. You take away nine of them. How many apples do you have now?
7. A driver was driving his truck on a broad highway. There was no moon. There were no lights. The truck's lights were also not working. Yet, the driver could see a woman crossing the road up ahead. How is this possible?
8. This thing can get rid of gloom and cold and yet needs a provocation to bloom. It spreads cheer, but when it blossoms beyond control, it can destroy ruthlessly. What is it?
9. A man was walking his dog and suddenly it started raining heavily. His clothes, his shoes, his bag, the dog and the dog's leash were all completely drenched. Yet, not one single strand of the man's hair got wet. How?
10. A man living in the US cannot be buried in the United Kingdom because ____________

ANSWERS QUIZ 36

1. The elephant's shadow
2. A mirror
3. Thunder
4. Everyone knows that before any game starts, the score is always 0-0
5. Few
6. 9 apples; the rest are in the bowl on the table
7. It was day time
8. Fire or flame
9. He was bald
10. The North Pole

QUIZ 37

1. What is heavier – a ton of cotton or a ton of iron?
2. This word contains all the 26 letters. Which word?
3. Name an honest musical instrument.
4. My first part is a word for dog and the second part a word for a monthly payment. I mean the present and I can also be found in a river.
5. What do bees say to flowers?
6. I fly without wings and I cry without tears. Who am I?
7. Teddy bears never ever feel hungry. Why?
8. These two rarely meet and most often come separately. When they do meet, these are the best moments of your life. Name the pair.
9. Yellow bricks are used to build yellow houses. Red bricks are used to build red houses. Blue bricks are used to build blue houses. What color bricks will be used to build a green house?
10. I only respond when spoken to. I don't speak on my own. What am I?

ANSWERS QUIZ 37

1. Both weigh the same – one ton
2. The alphabet
3. An upright piano
4. Current
5. Hey, honey!
6. Clouds
7. Because they are stuffed
8. Tears and smiles
9. A green house is always made of glass
10. An echo

QUIZ 38

1. A truck driver was going on a one-way street in the opposite direction. A traffic cop saw him and yet did nothing. How is it possible?
2. I am as hard as a rock. But the second you touch me, I begin to soften and soon can completely disappear. What am I?
3. I love hot water and I keep the water hot for a long time.
4. Tommy's mother had three children. Two of the children were named January and February. What do you think is the name of the third child?
5. I am something very closely related to everything in this world. I only move forward and there is no going back for me. What am I?
6. It repeats what you say even without ears and mouth.
7. If you need to use me, you have to first use me. What am I?
8. This creature is alive without breathing. It is as cold as death. It is never thirsty and yet is always drinking. What is it?
9. A boy was behaving badly in class and he was taken to the principal's office that said, "It wouldn't be fair for me to punish the boy as he is my son. I give you my permission to punish him suitably." But the principal was not the boy's mother. Is it possible?
10. I have no wings and yet I can soar. I can be wild and crazy. I can frighten even the strongest man. (Clue: I cannot be touched)

ANSWERS QUIZ 38

1. The truck driver was walking!
2. An ice cube
3. Hot water bottle
4. Tommy
5. Age
6. An echo
7. An egg
8. Fish
9. Yes, the principal was the boy's father
10. Imagination

QUIZ 39

1. Sometimes my tines are long and sometimes they are short. But my tines end before my report is submitted. What am I?
2. This has been around us for millions of years and yet it is not more than one month old.
3. You can enter it, but you cannot live on it. What am I talking about?
4. You have a bright blue satin ribbon that is 10 cm long and you love it with all your heart. But, you want to make it bigger without adding anything to it. How can you do it?
5. You need me to move forward. The more you move forward, the more of me you leave behind.
6. The higher I go, the hotter I get. I am stuck in my glass cage. What am I?
7. I run all around the city or home and yet I am unmoving.
8. This man turns left thrice after leaving home and returns home to find two masked men. What are we talking about?
9. This thing has a head and a tail. But, unfortunately, it has no head. We use it every day. What is it?
10. You are late returning from work and there is a power shutdown in your locality. Your home is dark and looks eerie. You fumble through your handbag and find a cigar, a small portable kerosene lamp, and a matchbox. You open the door and the room is cold as ever though the fireplace is filled with fresh wood. What will you light first?

ANSWERS QUIZ 39

1. Lightning
2. Moon
3. The 'enter' key on the keyboard
4. Place a smaller ribbon next to it. The blue one will look bigger
5. Footsteps
6. Mercury (in a thermometer)
7. Wall
8. Baseball game: the masked men are the umpire and the catcher
9. A coin
10. A matchstick

QUIZ 40

1. It runs and runs and does not ever stop. You can sometimes see it, but it never sees. It brings boredom when it is long and fear when it is short.
2. How can an island and the letter T be compared? Why are they both similar to each other?
3. What fur can you get from a tiger?
4. Imagine this. You see an electric car driving in the northern direction away from you. There is a southwesterly wind blowing in the same area? Which direction will the smoke from the car travel towards?
5. I pass right through the sun and yet do not make a shadow.
6. Two sons and two fathers go on a fishing expedition and each of them catches a fish. But they have only three fishes with them. How?
7. I am that alphabet that is silent when you ask a doubt to your teacher. Which alphabet am I?
8. Three men were rowing in a boat when suddenly there came a big storm and the boat capsized. Two men got their hair all wet. The third did not. How?
9. If everyone in the country bought white cars, what will we become?
10. What can hold water despite being full of holes?

ANSWERS QUIZ 40

1. Time
2. Both are in the middle of waTer.
3. As fur away as you can
4. Electric cars do not give out smoke
5. The wind
6. It was a threesome: grandfather, father and son. The father was a father and a son
7. B (silent in doubt)
8. He was bald
9. A white carnation
10. Sponge